DATE DUE

APR 1 5 2010	
AUG 1 6	

Mega Military Machines™
Megamáquinas militares™

TANKS

TANQUES

Catherine Ellis

Traducción al español: María Cristina Brusca

PowerKiDS press™ & **Editorial Buenas Letras**™

New York

Published in 2007 by The Rosen Publishing Group, Inc.
29 East 21st Street, New York, NY 10010

First Edition

Editor: Amelie von Zumbusch
Book Design: Greg Tucker
Layout Design: Lissette González

Photo Credits: Cover, p. 21 © Eugene Mogilnikov; p. 5 © Scott Nelson/Getty Images; p. 7 © Menahem Kahana/AFP/Getty Images; pp. 9, 15 © Larry W. Smith/Getty Images; p. 11 © Sgt. Paula Taylor; p. 13 © Spc. Danielle Howard; p. 17 Shutterstock.com; p. 19 © PHAN Sarah E. Ard, USN; p. 23 © Suzanne M. Day.

Cataloging Data

Ellis, Catherine.
    Tanks / Catherine Ellis; traducción al español: María Cristina Brusca. — 1st ed.
        p. cm. — (Mega military machines–Megamáquinas militares)
    Includes index.
    ISBN-13: 978-1-4042-7619-2 (library binding)
    ISBN-10: 1-4042-7619-X (library binding)
    1. Tanks (Military science)—Juvenile literature. 2. Spanish language materials I. Title.

Manufactured in the United States of America

Contents

Contenido

People in the military drive tanks. They use tanks to fight and to move around.

En el ejército, los soldados manejan tanques. Los tanques se usan para pelear y para viajar.

Tanks have **tracks**. A tank's tracks let it be driven on or off the road.

Los tanques tienen bandas llamadas **orugas.** Las orugas les permiten avanzar por dentro y fuera de los caminos.

Tanks are strong. They have **armor** on their sides to keep them safe.

Los tanques son muy fuertes. Los tanques tienen **blindaje** a los lados. El blindaje los hace muy seguros.

Tanks have guns on them.
The guns on tanks are often
very big.

Los tanques tienen armas.
Con frecuencia, las armas de
los tanques son muy grandes.

Soldiers ride inside of a tank. They sometimes sit so that they can look out of the top of the tank.

Los soldados viajan dentro de los tanques. A veces, se asoman por arriba del tanque para vigilar los alrededores.

13

This tank is called a Bradley tank. It lets soldiers move around safely.

Este tipo de tanque se llama Bradley. Los Bradley protegen a los soldados cuando viajan.

This is an M1A1 Abrams tank. The U.S. Army uses a lot of M1A1 Abrams tanks.

Este es un tanque M1A1 Abrams. El ejército de Estados Unidos utiliza muchos tanques M1A1 Abrams.

All tanks can be driven on land. Some tanks can go into the water, too!

Todos los tanques pueden andar por la tierra. ¡Algunos tanques también pueden andar por el agua!

Tanks come in many sizes.
This small tank can hold
three soldiers.

Hay tanques de muchos
tamaños. Este pequeño
tanque puede llevar a
tres soldados.

Tanks are often part of a **platoon**. There are three or four tanks in each platoon.

Muchas veces, los tanques son parte de un **pelotón**. En cada pelotón hay tres o cuatro tanques.

armor (AR-mer) A hard cover put over something to keep it safe.

platoon (PLUH-toon) A small military group.

tracks (TRAKS) The heavy bands that move a tank along.

---

blindaje (el) Una cubierta dura que se pone sobre una cosa para protegerla.

orugas (las) Bandas pesadas que mueven los tanques.

pelotón (el) Un pequeño grupo militar.